Me and A Moment

jennskies teachworth

ISBN: 978-0-9968648-3-1

for my younger self,
who really needed a book like this

&

for Marianne
for Molly
for Lauren
for Rochelle

&
most of all,
for Mr. Lucky & Lucille Simone

CONTENTS

ME AND A MOMENT AT WORK.

My main work outlines a cube
In dimensions near the site of a third eye

I pay my whole mind
To work and rework it

Still, every time I laugh
About the elbow in my spine

DO Y'ALL NEED ROOM FOR CREAM?

a mish-mash of a schedule with a first alarm
around last call at the bars
punching the four AM clock can be dreadful
my route to work lit by stars

the risks for oversleeping: a barista befallen exhaustion
a phone left on silent
rivals those other thrills and risks that
would make this job impossible for keeping

"you are far too brilliant," my father admits
"to be pouring people's coffees!"
—then I've lost him again

caffeine withdrawal migraine on the mind?
cabstand is without a line?
makes a meeting with diversity
and people who are kind
early mornings met with such adoration
blessings for our refusal to submit
to Mr. Sandman's bags of optical abrasion—
as though for sleep he arrives with a writ

maybe through talking to people
who are standing idly by,
we are able to actually learn
a little more deeply the true agonies
of those who need support
like understanding humanity
through building rapport

those lessons
are irrevocably life-sustaining: permanence
of wisdom adding to the hourly gaining
so
maybe this "decision" of mine

to really study the human condition
instead of a fast-tracked MBA
from an accredited institution
is to find value where others may find only spite
like to write my hindsight

though not without bitterness benders
where my outlook goes askew;
fearing my turn as one of those pretenders
where nothing of my self is true

though feeling heard in Real Time when
speaking truth taught Time how to tame them
like these thoughts
spanning a walk to work
lit by stars

KNEELING NEVER MADE SENSE TO ME.

it wasn't the Wednesday after Mardi Gras
but my soul fell
like ashes to the ground

in three languages,
I can Hail Mary
with His Bible shut
words lacking belief
neglect of our Magdalene
(all too familiar sounds)

born bred educated fed
on the command of the Pope
Catholic Marks
a sling like stinging
less like her Harp
his liturgical symphony of fear—
silent sermons serving judgment
without my consent
"Catholic guilt,"
I've heard it called
and this woman's soul,
the one that Dogma mauled

I cherished the discipline—
it's likely all I could believe in

Mother Mary,
it must have been so hard

"When did you stop believing in God?"
as if it were reductive
or something so finite
if I had simply stopped believing,
would it still keep me up at night?
the self worth tension

stinging measurements
calculated via Doctrine

then
finding Edna
realizing
I never was one to fit in
with those exclusivist types

REMEMBER TO YELL "HELP!" BEFORE DROWNING.

a funny thing is the memory
of the who and of the why
and of these the humor lies
in my chosen avoidance

they barge in during sleep, contaminating dreams
like that fallen fly in the mason jar
(half-full of wine, on my nightstand)

dream
can feel like flying blissfully
through an illuminated night sky
just like Peter Pan
unless you're more like me where
memory and
dream
just feels like a sewer dwelling
or it feels like those scraps of trash
clogging gutter grates   causing flooding

memories where
death of the self is wholesale
   every single night another flood forges forward

before a boat and before an oar
I couldn't make peace with the tide
so I built a boat with my own hands
 following some Paint by Number directions

when the tide gets high
and I've gone out to sea
   these terrors of dreams flow like floods

PANIC PLAYED ME LIKE A FOOL.

a jolt just above my rib cage,
where a freeway of emotions merges in my chest
        it's a blunt-force blow, powered with cloaked rage,
like a foot stomping out breath; like mimicking cardiac arrest
        rib cage network collapses and
        lethargy bottles of conflicting emotions
        their conflicts? the weight of Panic's rage, perhaps
too major a network jam to move through
        without some mental confusion and sense of delusion
a visceral freeway built upon inner truths
        and then Panic blankets, making clear Her objectives
        send out an *SOS!* to therapist,
        my emotional sleuth
        who holds most qualified perspectives
        for such a high stakes pursuit
even an emotional freeway emergency shoulder
        cannot control contraflows
        especially with an automatic transmission
        on a loop paved with irrational insecurities
        lacking enough awareness to find a way out
        that's not already fucked up
automatic and repeating, bumper to bumper—
        thoughts getting stuck

Panic's hands rarely release her grip: your heart is her clutch
emotions racing each other
        trying to be seen in first place
all I feel is numb
        like needing my mother
instead, an orange bottle holds my hand
        and strokes my face
                orange bottles carrying first responders:
prescribed to sedate entire networks of emotional freeways
        so neurons firing no longer have their previous priorities
        in a cocoon of yellow caution tape, I sigh
send everyone home—the evening's caput
        and on Tuesday we'll recite

another thorough incident report
if safety is supposed to make me feel better,
why does each ingestion go down like defeat?
like embodiment as perpetual debtor,
day after day, another Panic Jam stuck on repeat

can I enjoy the calm from safely behind these closed and caution-taped frames?
space for mental wandering is easier to find when first responders play in Panic's game
that little white pill and then Panic melts;
belittled, gnawing, irritating anxiety whose scorn pelts
readying to return; but when?

COULDN'T FIND HER IN THEIR PRAYERS.

gravel is just rocks
like asphalt but broken apart
here we stand at the middle edge
paying no mind to ticking hands
words like weaponry
an arsenal of adjectives
with emotions in fragments
rooms with old views
of feigned appetites
of thoughts perverse

fought a fire fainting
fell in love dying and
never found god praying

IN BETWEEN THE MISSION AND MYSELF.

a spring in haze
we might say about this one time (maybe a Tuesday)
when people forget their names
and become their selves
(not those physical kinds
like bodies built for a trophy's shelf)

become beings of full minds
on paths led by truths
rather than clearings full of mines

with fleeing, a pounding
freeing
a stern feeling just below the sternum
of a fast-paced beating

the entire day just recounting itself in systole

SOME TIMES IN THIS STREET FIGHT.

a moment of clarity starts to end
the pangs of humiliation return with a greater frequency
and volume (like right now)
now is when my breath is getting even
more shallow
but I'm doing all the moves I know to keep it as deep as possible
I start to go away and
usually I would hit cancel
twice
but I'm going to hit send
instead
I'm going to try to stay present
talking to you via this blank composition
because I don't want to go away right now
don't want to make myself feel humiliated or disconnected
only so this spectacle called
"life: the inner narrative"
will go on
I want to be able to skip that step;
that step is so maladaptive—it physically hurts

I want to just stay here talking to you
and remembering that in this street fight:
the opponents have a lot of masks,
    and sometimes they look like our own selves

I'VE READ TOO MUCH EMILY DICKINSON.

my naïveté his object
for clarification
his foul
play

in many mornings after the Surrender
I may as well have had
my head in an Emily Dickinson book
reading all the ways I could express
such distaste of feeling him
still stuck in my gut

but instead,
I drifted my descent down curved stairs
to my father in the kitchen
I held out to him my bowl,
full with milked cereal:
"Dad! I no longer like milk. It has become another thing I suddenly cannot stand!"

thought their daughter may be missing
maybe misbehaving

considered her face on milk cartons
that Old School approach
what if someone had just asked
"hey, girl, you doin' okay?"

moments of remembering surrendering
eliminates essential life-affirming abilities
including remembering
self
worth
or
how sound waves carry
what existence felt like
before it always felt like
the presumptuous moment before drowning

right after the ironic gasp before going under

so when I remember my first,
I don't get nostalgic or sentimental—
I get panic and I get accidental,
self-conscious, emotionally avoidant

girl thought she held no value
when he had taken it by force
and

instead of walking away from it,
I count more years
dragging a cross
those cobbled rocks
that created that road
that destroyed that girl

I cannot forget.

I remember
what living was like:
sleeping with Dread and
rising a member of the Undead

his scowl—
those threats—
the dark-watered ditch—
because when my body remembers
she feels dismembered
and I have to remember
this body
afraid again
just like me,
age thirteen

TAKE ME TO MY LAUGHING PLACE.

doom as epic, doom as natural:
a disaster.
doom as female, by name
but demon of demise
she was full of dirty water and took over home so that when home was no more,
safety and security were also no more

dirty water stained the new horizon I gained:
family in an apartment where, before,
furniture had been living alone
but now, crying on the couch,
is a robe with a mother inside;

a robe with a mother inside and
a suitcase with clothes for a daughter outside
a hero hiding behind a father with tears on a tarmac and
a tarmac with tears because of a daughter with fears
a castle with floors, doors, halls—a great place
    my hand, I offered to shake an introduction
    "come on, we can give hugs here,"
    said mister kent jones with
    such a heart-warming induction

I found a best friend, a Brynn
a friend with a tickling grin
chuckles upping my chin
a place with space for laughing

down the hall with giddy pace
a yearbook letter
cover to cover and
granted a lifetime award
to that ship I had never before been the best on

take me to that laughing place

TO THINK AND TO BE THOUGHTFUL.

I sit below She's trees,
thinking thoughts to find
logic in life and in His fees
I ration some Benjamin Franklin
and I ration some Socrates
I thought up a trail near Godot's last stop
when
Thinking thought,
"perhaps I should fail, perhaps I ought not"

sitting below She's trees
imposing logical thinking upon dimensions veiled
here we go, says Opaque
while I'm drifting into the existential
in my existence, Life's meaning, I lived to find—
I lived and I died, over and over in my mind
a truth told like we speak and you love us

because art moves people who are standing still
before I met you I was as dead as I was ill

my effort for virtue:
unseen it will continue going
so long as your gaze
is the only Other of me showing

to think and to be thoughtful,
like those virtues of the humble
so think and be thoughtful, visit the trail by the trees

to know thyself
is to have thought things through
to think when Other would stagnate;
to be me—even with you

and with you is like
art moving me
and Being entirely
still

THANK YOU FOR SHARING YOUR FRIENDS.

*for heather christle

i.
the trees the trees making sugar all the time
I barked my frustrations
carved my way inside
made some real weight
threw it out with older scraps
composted self-resignation knotted
to the life disguised in the experience of the boldly embarked

ii.
those men are here again demanding dates   they never believe me
they chop me down
again and again count my insides over and over
(concentric
deductions)
chucked at the core for
two divisions
wood for nailing wood for burning

iii.
an entire forest!
the trees understand
the trees know my handwriting
how it comes together
like strokes
resembling my mother's
the trees can hold so many things,
 like a story
I once wrote and
in it I was a tree too

IN BETWEEN THE MISSION AND SOUND.

overcast sky like a cookie sheet of gray
shadows of hands---
like shapes without Proper Names
reaching up and
carving out pieces for self
in the name of Peace
drowning in densities of dreams

how did they get so far above us anyway?
(maybe hollow insides)

left you where they show us how to cry
even ate my lunch on top of you
it is also where they help us with things
like tying our shoelaces in the daytime

how to become the embodiment of life
before mailing a ballot for death
like these lungs have a capacity
for holding air
even when it is of a breathless room
where motivation is stale

BECOMING

like a body of water
fluidity a natural component
there is no shoreline
where I end I also begin
before I inundated an area
like taking the space
I was, I am
a particle finding energy in connection
the hydrogen that makes this human matter
bonding, the oxygen where your words
walk in &
then a breath &
then a life

ALCHEMY

the six-word memoir has long held my attentions
an outlet for tension drawing from simplistic adaptations

if myth is where the truth has been hidden
then all we continue to create
is rebuilding what has been destroyed

ACKNOWLEDGMENTS

This book is the product of years working on my tendency to prevent anything from coming to fruition if it hadn't somehow attained perfection. This book is the result of academic mentors, mental health professionals, and my former "regulars" at a major coffee shop – all of whom believed in my abilities enough to support this project, either through monetary donations, encouragement, emotional support, or conversation.

The Emma Willard School generously provided for me during some of the most pivotal moments of my life. I am infinitely grateful for the generosity of the education and the safe haven that you provided me immediately after Hurricane Katrina in 2005. You taught me so much more than any syllabus could outline and wanted nothing in return except for my continued curiosity in this world. Your kindness has instilled in me the purpose of being generous and kind with the world. Thank you.

Kent Jones, Mark van Wormer, Heidi Makoutz, thank you.

I would be remiss if I did not mention the impact that music has had on my life. Tori Amos, thank you for sharing your song girls. They have provided me with guidance, solace, love, and a sense of belonging ever since a chance viewing of your performance on the Conan O'Brien show in the late 1990s.

www.ingramcontent.com/pod-product-compliance
Lightning Source LLC
LaVergne TN
LVHW010842120826
845149LV00020B/3491